Title

BLIND, BUT NOW I SEE!

(A Story of Pain and Sacrifice)

This book is dedicated to Veronica & Courtney

ACKNOWLEDGMENTS:

FIRST AND FOREMOST, I THANK GOD FOR HIS GRACE AND MERCY. I WOULD ALSO LIKE TO THANK MY CHILDREN FOR THEIR PATIENCE AND TO OFFER A SINCERE APOLOGY. THIS BOOK IS A HEALING TOOL FOR ME. THE KEY TO HEALING IS FORGIVENESS. FORGIVE EVERYONE WHO HAS TAKEN SOMETHING AWAY FROM YOU BECAUSE AFTER YOU DO, GOD WILL GIVE IT ALL BACK.

Chapter One

Summer 1970

I have often wondered what it would have been like to grow up in a loving home, a home filled with a family that prayed together and had a father who was being led by God. Unfortunately, I did not grow up in that kind of home; instead my upbringing was a horror movie. My story begins at the innocent age of nine. I watched my father drag a woman's body down a flight of concrete stairs. The sound of her voice yelling and screaming still haunts me even now. My siblings looked on from inside the front door and began to cry at the cruel act that took place in the front yard. My father then left this fragile body bleeding on the ground, ran back into the house, picked up the telephone, and made a very important call.

The person on the other end of that call was a lady of dignity and honor, but the words that she heard exposed heart break. The neighbors watched this terrible act. We were crying and screaming for help. He was like a mad dog gone wild, and I don't know what set him off. The evil in his eyes scared my siblings and I to the point of hysterics. No one tried to stop this crazy man from hurting this woman. He ranted and raged with such a fury that it reminded me of a movie I once watched called *The Chainsaw Massacre.* Only this was real life, and it happened right before my eyes. It was so horrible that words can't describe it. I thought she was going to die at the hands of my father that day. I was only nine years old, and my siblings were much younger.

We cried so much that day until I know that anger hides most of our pain. That day alone has kept me in bondage. I have retained so many harmful feelings from that one day. The thought of it has taken the very breath from my body. All of the

screaming still rings out in my mind, and I can hear the blood

boiling sounds of her voice. I see faces filled with fear and the

heart racing courage that it took to accept that cruel act. The

audacity of this man handling a helpless woman down to the

ground, as if she was a match for him, is insane. A man that

would put his hands on a woman in anger is a coward and has

no courage. The fight did not just end there. When my father

made that call, little did he know that the local authorities

would be on their way to our home.

Chapter two

The woman being abused was my mother. She had a sweet

face with a heart of gold. I'm sure that she did not sign up to

participate in a boxing match, although her daily activity

became a ring side attraction. Instead of living in a white house with a picket fence, one might say, her home was more like a dungeon with black walls and skeletons lying all around. A family member came to help out, subsequently; she was the voice at the other end of the phone. She was a short, stout woman with long, gray hair. She never owned a driver's license or a car for that matter;therefore, she walked everywhere. She walked all over the city with a stick in one hand and an umbrella in the other. The stick was for the neighborhood dogs. Sometimes if it was too far to walk, she would take a taxi cab, but this particular day I believed she ran all the way to our house. The authorities took my father away. He spent the night in jail. Meanwhile, we were home trying to put our emotions back in tack. This angel of mercy, known as

my Grandmama, made something good to eat as she would

normally do. We all sat close to her on the couch and watched

a movie on the television. She went home before night fall. By

the time mama awoke from her nap, there was a knock on the

door and after I opened it, there stood Ma'dear.

Ma'dear was a woman with a sad demeanor and an

unconcerned mannerism. The look on her face, as if no one

was home, was filled with coldness all the time. I felt unloved

whenever I was in the same room with her. She came to our

home and wanted to know what happened. My mother

explained that my father had dragged her body, as if she was a

rag doll, down a flight of stairs. My father's mother, Ma'dear, began to laugh as if she was joking. I could not understand the laughter because there was no humor in what was said. I knew that Ma'dear should have had some type of empathy with the story because my grandfather would do the same to her.

As I look back over the years, I guess the laughter took the place of tears. My father was the epitome of his father. He was a sad skeleton of a man. He was mean spirited, and anger led his path each day. Daddy Buster was his world and parent that he looked to for guidance. His mistreatment of Ma'dear taught my father how to be violent. The whole family was given a lesson on how to fight. All the siblings in the household completed a course in how to speak nasty words to each other and how to hit first, then laugh later. I witnessed on various holidays the acts of violence that my grandfather gave

out to his family. Holidays were always filled with confusion.

I can't remember a time that love or affection was ever shown.

They never gave any gifts or spent any time with my siblings

and me. The only thing they gave was a hole in my heart.

A hole that grew so large it began to eat at my soul. I

became bitter at my father as the years went by. I thought he

was a monster for all the terrible things he said and did. My

father would hit in a fit of rage whenever he drank too much.

He became so violent that it didn't even matter if we were in

the same room with him or if company was visiting.

Sometimes the abuser is not controlled by an addition, but is

taught how to be angry. He mimics what he sees in the

household. My father would even ask us to get out of our home. "How could we leave?" I would say to myself. "This is our home too." When we did leave, our only choice was to stay with grandparents. A four room house not large enough to turn around in was all that they had. We slept on hardwood floors. Seven of us all nested together covered by one homemade quit. They would put out the fire before bedtime, and I would be very cold. Grandmama only kept the fire burning during the day because the stove burned wood.

Chapter three

My mother's parents were very spiritual people, and they did a lot of praying. My Grandmama was a member of the neighborhood church. She stood firm in her belief, and prayer was the answer to all of her problems. She always talked about her parents and how their love served as a strong weapon that held the family together. She would reprimand me and my siblings for calling each other ugly names. She said they never spoke to each other in such a manner in the home that she grew up in. My grandparents were church abiding souls that taught discipline with a finger of love. She was a strong woman infused with a power to love everyone. She knew no strangers and embraced everyone that crossed her path. Although she never worked a full time job, she worked hard in her home.

I was blessed to have her around, and the training that she gave me was completely from her heart. She loved me unconditionally with every breath in her body. And so did my

grandfather who was a Baptist minister. They went their

separate ways on Sunday morning, but at the end of the day,

only love and peace was shared in their home. Their home,

although small, was very large in spirit and always filled with

delicious home cooked meals. It was our safe haven from the

boogie man. My grandfather never knew his parents. And

although, he did not grow up with as many siblings as I did, he

was a free hearted soul. He would give and give until he had

nothing left.

Every visit that we made to my grandparents' home was

always a great joy. I never regretted the time that I spent with

them. My grandfather never learned to read or write. I

thought it was funny when he would sign his name with an X.

Now, it makes me sad to know that he could not go to school

because he had to work in the fields to put food in his

household. My grandparents often told the story of how they

met and got married. They were the sweetest couple you

would ever want to meet. I would watch them give each other

pedicures. Grandfather was a good man. He always

demonstrated the true meaning of love.

Chapter four

In my father's house it was just the opposite. Alcoholic drinks

were the spirit that controlled our house and his father's house

as well. They used to drink until no end, which turned them

into demons. In my father's house there were many secrets, lies, and physical violence. He was also committed to more than one marriage. I didn't understand that until I got a little older. How degraded and misused it made me feel. So I could only dream of how it made my mother feel. She went through some very trying times with my father. I know that it made her strong, but we all have our breaking points.

I know in some countries it is legal to be married to more than one woman. The secrets that my father kept were cruel and inhumane like the fact that he married another woman while he was still married to my mother. This is against the law in this country. I watched my mother read the marriage announcement in the newspaper and began to cry so pitifully as her heart broke into many pieces. I don't remember how old I was, but I was old enough to understand that something was wrong. The woman he married worked for the same company as my mother. Were they friends at some point or just co-workers? I never knew the answer because my mother does not speak about the event. I can't blame her because it's too painful to even remember. She had to face this woman day after day. I wonder what went on in the other woman's mind. Did she know that my father already had a wife? These questions will never get answered now because it's too late. What thrill does a man get from having two marriages and both women expecting at the same time?

When the newborn came, her mother would bring the baby

to Ma'dear's house to visit. My siblings and I would fight over

who would get to hold this beautiful baby, a little girl who

looked just like my Dad. Of course we didn't know that the

baby was related to us, and we were fighting over our own

sister. I overheard my granddaddy (Daddy Buster) say, "My

son has two wives and that makes him a better man than me."

He laughed out loud cracking joke after joke about the

situation. He was a sick man to condone such behavior, and I

understand why my father acted as he did. He was looking for

approval from his father.

I'm not sure how long that marriage lasted, but my father

managed to come back into our lives. We moved to another

neighborhood into a lovely little house. My mother just stepped back into her role of being his better half and punching bag. How could she have a love for this man? He was sick in his mind, and so was she in order to allow all of the bad things that took place in and out of our home.

When my father would leave us for weeks at a time, my mother would be frightened to be home without him. She would wake me up from my sleep, and we would watch TV. Or she would make me draw a picture in order for me to stay awake. Sometimes she would give me a slice of pie or cookies to keep me from falling back to sleep. Other times we stayed up all night and would watch the sun come up the next morning. She would sit on the couch with the front door open

and me right by her side.

Chapter five

I believed she got very ill one day because our home was

never the same. If you can define the term nervous breakdown,

that's what happened. It was like being at a funeral. The air in

each room of the house felt cold, and it was too quiet and

discouraging, with fear filling each corner. There were no

domestic violence laws that I was aware of. How could I

know? I was only a minor. It was up to the strangers to set the

rules and make decisions for my family's disagreements.

My father's temper and harsh treatment often caused financial hardship. There was never enough food, and we often went to bed hungry. One day mother sat quietly in a chair with tears running down her face. I'm sure that my father had moved away to be with another woman because we didn't have any food to eat. The person that I called mama said softly that she didn't know what we were going to do. I told her to ask the store merchant for some credit.

There was a neighborhood store that she sent me to frequently. I went to the store, gave the owner a note, and asked if my family could have the items on credit. And his reply was, "I don't know your family." I said that I understood and as I began to walk away he said, "But I do know you." He filled the list and said, "Your mother can pay me on Friday." I went home with the bag of groceries, and everyone was so excited, it brought smiles to their faces. I was negotiating for my father in order to put food on our table.

As I lay in my bed each night, I would think about the day, what transpired and wondered when it all would end. As soon as I thought that it was safe to close my eyes, my father would come home in a drunken rage and snatch me from my bed to clean the kitchen although it was already clean. Then he would wake up the entire house knowing we had school the next day. He had a mean, selfish, and arrogant spirit. Once I saw him hit one of my sibling's in the face with an electric heater. Sadly, all we could do was just stand back and watch.

Understandably, fright took over our minds and bodies. There were many times that I just wanted to leave.

Why was I born into this family? I would meet girls my age with parents who gave them love and attention. My father would yell bad words at me in front of my friends. My friends had their own bedrooms, and they wore pretty clothes to school. Some had braces on their teeth, and I had never been to a dentist. Their fathers picked them up from school in nice cars, and I had to walk for miles. Their parents were waiting for them when they got home with dinner already prepared. I, on the other hand, was responsible for cooking the meals for the entire family. I had to make sure school clothes were ironed and help my siblings with their homework. If I asked for help with my homework, my father would call me a dummy

or say that I was too ignorant to learn.

I often felt like a parent to my parents. I was responsible for

my siblings and took care of their needs. I have always felt

like the adult with the role of babysitter and housekeeper

especially during the summer months when school let out.

When we all passed to the next grade, I had to make sure we

got registered at our new schools. Sometimes when we did go

to new schools, it was kind of scary and there was a lot of

uncertainty. We never had the support of a parent to make us

feel secure. I didn't make friends easily because I was shy and

slow to speak. I had been taught that a child is meant to be

seen and not heard. Mother and Grandmama would scold us

severely for speaking out in front of company or even being in

the same room. It gave me a severe complex, and I always felt

like I didn't fit in everywhere I went. I'd had enough, but

didn't know what to do or where to turn.

Chapter six

She was always upset about something, and I felt bad because

I did not know how to fix the problem. Not knowing, it wasn't

my responsibility to fix in the first place. When she did pull

herself out of bed, she would just sit around in her pajamas

looking depressed. She had her hair in rollers and an evil look

on her face that melted my heart. She became just as negative

as my father and never had a kind word to say. I took on her household chores in the home full time. It didn't feel right, and I now know that it wasn't right. I don't believe I experienced my youth from young eyes. We never ate out or went to movies, and a family vacation was out of the question.

My father never stopped cheating. He moved in with another woman. In the meantime, his father, Daddy Buster, died. On the day of the funeral we were all gathered in Ma'dear's living room. She and my family members were acting very strange. At the time, I didn't know they were hiding my father's mistress in one of the bedrooms.

Why did my mother subject herself and all of us to that scene? There was no law that said we had to go to my grandfather's funeral. He had never been in our lives, and the times that I did see him turned bad from his controlling, violent temper. He never accepted me as his granddaughter, but I forgave him for his shortcomings. It took me a long time to forgive him. His rude manners and bad language made me harsh, and I didn't think that I could love myself or anyone that I came in contact with.

I couldn't express the feelings that went on inside of me because I had no one to talk to. I can tell you now that it made me sick to my stomach, and for years I suffered with stomach problems. It was brought on by stress, violent fights, and a fear of everything and everyone. I disliked my father even more for years, and I know that it was wrong. My feelings were inappropriate for the man who bought me into this world. I was really in a bad place mentally and physically, but I didn't know to what degree the drama in our household had crippled me.

After a few weeks had passed and my father was tired of playing house with his mistress, he decided to come back home. Time and time again my mother kept accepting him back into our lives bringing on more problems. Nothing had changed. He was still the cruel and controlling individual that kept me on pins and needles. I wonder did he treat the other women in his life that way. Did he hit them and use abusive words so easily that it diminished their self-worth?

On an average day in our home, if my father wasn't there, I was content with all the work that I had to do. I could have friends over, but not often, only if the atmosphere was good. I could share fun times, but when my father came home, his presence made me tense. I would walk around the house as if I were invisible. I would say to myself, "Lord please don't let him notice me, hit me, or yell at me today." He often called me ugly names in front of my friends.

I had just walked into the house with a friend. My father came into the living room and had not turned to see me standing at the front door. He yelled, "Where's Angie, that witch?" His face turned red when he saw my friend standing beside me. I'm sure he didn't want that secret known that he would use such language when referring to me. Why would he call me such a name? I was so embarrassed and afraid that he would try to hit me in front of my friends until I decided that I wouldn't invite anyone over to our house. I had a very special friend with whom I became very close. We often prayed together. He was so patient with me and accepted all of my troubles. He never asked any questions, and I became very dependent on him. I was so needy and clingy that I felt he would stop being my friend. I tried to spend a lot of time at his home, but his parents would often complain. My friend started working at a restaurant. I wasn't old enough to work there, but the manager allowed me to do so for a short time. I would call my friend to pick me up from work, and I could hear his

mother in the background saying, "Where is her father?"

I worked to help my mother buy school clothes for my

siblings. I also paid bills that sometimes included the mortgage

payment, utilities and groceries. I once bought a washer and

dryer for our home because I was sick of going to the

laundromat. We hung the clothes outside on a clothesline to

allow them to dry in the sun. My parents were very hard on

me, but as years went by, the younger kids got away with a lot

more. While looking back in time, I can only remember the

bad times that controlled a large portion of my emotions.

Chapter seven

The holiday season would bring on a different type of celebration. For instance, Christmas day was supposed to be filled with joy and happiness. My holiday would turn into *Nightmare on Elm Street*. My father would invite his friends over, and they would get intoxicated and start to fight. The Christmas tree would get knocked down and our toys destroyed in the process. Sometimes we didn't receive anything at all for Christmas because there was no money to buy gifts. My father was a very proud man and never wanted any charity. Once one of my siblings sent a letter to Santa Claus, and the salvation army delivered a box of pre-owned toys to our home. My father went through the roof, and he punished her for sending the letter. I heard a preacher say that being proud is a trick of the devil and that you have to humble yourself. When pride

rules, it causes dishonesty.

Although there was not much money for food, clothing, and

Christmas presents, there was always money for alcoholic

drinks. Large bottles of gin, whiskey, and wine were placed

under the Christmas tree before any gifts. My mother never

disagreed with these actions. She never had an encouraging

word about our home life. I never saw her spiritual side until

she would pay a visit to church. She only yelled, screamed,

and belittled the situation. I often thought that she was just

mean, but I realize that she took all of her frustrations out on

her children. We were the weakest link, and she would lash

out at us as if we were the problem.

She had nothing left to give because my father had taken it all. He took her spirit, her smile, and her ability to love. My mother is still filled with anger, but she won't admit it. Her heart is still broken because she won't let go of the past. She has blocked out all of the ugly pictures and shame that took place. One winter night my father went out drinking with the guys. Anger was the main emotion in our home for decades.

A large amount of snow had fallen earlier in the day and by night fall, it had frozen. Now, he left in a car with his buddies, but came back walking. He rang the doorbell with such aggression that I was afraid to open the door. When I did open it, there he stood with one shoe on and the other one was missing. He limped into the house, and I was afraid to speak. I didn't know what happened to his shoe or why he was walking.

I can only imagine that he got into another drunken brawl and

ran out without it.

On another occasion, my father and his uncle were wearing

the same brown leather jacket. They were both inebriated and

began to argue about which jacket belong to whom. The

dispute became so huge that they were getting ready to throw

punches. Why was almost every one of my father's family

members so consumed by alcohol? My grandmother would

say, "Don't you kids drink alcohol because we have too many

drunks in the family already."

The only refuge I had was church. No one there knew the pain and suffering that I went through in my home. I sang in the choir and performed in many plays. I went to Sunday school and stayed for evening services only to keep from going home. Our choir was very active and went out to participate in other church services. One day my Grandmama said to me, "Angie, you must give your life to the Lord." I really didn't know what she meant because I was in church every time the doors opened already. She said, "Pray and ask the master to take control." I did pray, but it seemed that I wasn't being heard.

I would cry myself to sleep at night praying that the Lord would hear my cry and wipe away my tears. If I could jump in the river or take an entire bottle of pills then maybe all the hurt

and pain would go away. I was too afraid to try that because I

thought that God would not forgive me. There was nothing

another human being could do to help me. There were several

times that God saved my life, and I could not see it until now.

I always ate Sunday morning breakfast at my Grandmama's

house, and I told her that I was ready to join church. She asked

me if I had prayed about it and I said, "No, but it's time."

Grown-ups at my church seemed nice and so concerned, but

the kids my age were mean and evil. I never bonded with any

of them, and they never accepted me.

Chapter Eight

They never accepted me or that's how I felt thirty years ago. I felt like they looked down on me because I didn't have nice clothes to wear and my mother didn't send me to the beauty shop to get my hair done. I never fit in, and I was scared that someone there knew my secret. The secret was my father didn't love me. I thought the church was supposed to be a place of refuge where I could find kindness. I trusted people in the church because I thought that they loved me, but I later found out that it was just filled with unsaved souls, who had not been transformed. They were like ice with smiles frozen across their faces but hearts filled with pain. I could only see what people wanted me to see.

I was very sheltered from reality and had not experienced anything other than abuse. I was never taught to grow up, and maybe that was because my father never grew up. He never accepted his responsibilities as a father with seven children. Someone always had to clean up his mess. I didn't understand how your parents could disappoint you so bad. They are supposed to prepare you for the challenges that are forthcoming as you grow.

I do understand that people can be so transparent, and I experienced a very painful confrontation with a fellow church member. It was a scene out of a movie. She walked up to me and called me a liar over something she had heard someone else say. You know that "he said", "she said" stuff. I was shocked that an older woman with such grace and dignity could act that way. She floored me with her attitude and the words that came out of her mouth because she had been someone that I had looked up too. It's funny how people can change your persona of them in a blinking of an eye. I understood that day why my father didn't go to church. If you are not strong in your faith, those so called "Christian People" will eat you alive.

I never saw that in my grandmama. She was a pillar of strength and her faith was as strong as an elephant. She was the glue that kept my family together. If it had not been for her, I don't know how we would have survived. I loved my grandparents for all of their teachings, prayers, and availability to me. I spent a lot of time walking with them to many places to do things such as pay bills and shop for groceries. My grandmama would visit the sick, and I went along with her, carrying food and a word from the Lord. Little did I know that she was molding me into the woman that I am today. She taught me to have grace and dignity. I learned to have discernment for people and their problems. I could care about everyone, good or bad, because my grandparents showed only love to my father even through the drama that was performed daily. They accepted and loved him for who he was. The horrible acts were never repeated in their home, and not one harsh word was spoken against him. Although it was justified, I never heard anything but love.

My grandmama passed away shortly after I gave birth to my first child. She had a stroke and was paralyzed on the left side of her body. When we got her to the emergency room, she was cheerful and very talkative. She always made mention to the fact that she had one daughter and seven grandchildren. My mother was her pride and joy. Grandmama was on her way to heaven singing the praises of her daughter's accomplishments: the fact that she had brought seven babies into this world. Her prayer was that the Lord didn't allow her to suffer so that she wouldn't be a burden on her family.

My mother came from such a loving background that it confuses me greatly how she allowed us to live in the manner that we did. My father was always drunk, in between jobs, and waiting on an unemployment check. There was a time when he regained employment and was still receiving the checks. The court ordered him to repay the money. When he didn't comply with the judge's order he was given jail time. He had to serve 11 months and 29 days. He was incarcerated and given work detail outside of the correctional center. His job was to deliver goods to a store and one day he veered from his route and came home. There was a knock on the door and I opened it. It was my dad and he gave me the biggest smile & hug that I have ever had from him. He didn't stay long and we found out later that he had gotten drunk and wrecked the truck. His work detail was revoked and he had to do extra time for that incident. You would think a man, with responsibilities, would stop blaming everybody else for his problems and take ownership at some point in time.

My siblings and I sometimes discuss our upbringing, and we laugh to keep from crying. The stories sound so unbelievable until I wonder why I am still alive. For example, we never went to the doctor. If we got sick or hurt, then home remedies was given to solve the problem. I stepped on a nail and hurt my foot, which became so infected that I could barely walk on it. My mother placed a piece of pork meat on it and tied it up with a rag. I always had severe nose bleeds and a cough that I just couldn't shake. I was given a large spoon of castor oil and half of an orange. One of my siblings had nose bleeds that lead to severe fever and body aches. Mother would place ice packs on his body to reduce the fever. Another fell from the top bunk bed and hit his eye on a bed post before landing on the floor. His eye closed up and was as large as a golf ball. No medical attention was given to any of these situations but we are all still alive. I assumed that my parents didn't have medical coverage or just couldn't afford it.

Although my father was rude and disrespectful more times than not, he would show some affection and kindness during these times. I saw him give my mother a few gifts on occasions. I remember it was her birthday; he gave her a diamond ring and a dozen roses. Once he gave her a giant box of valentine candy with a nice card.

One might ask the question how they managed to have seven children if all they did was fight. My father decorated the entire house each year with new furnishings without my mother's input. I could see the disappointment on her face time and time again. She wouldn't even know that the furniture was coming until it was being delivered.

Chapter nine

Holidays were always *Showtime at the Apollo,* and my father was the star. One Easter Holiday, we ate all of the candy, and my father paddled us for eating it. I'm sure we ate it because we were hungry. He brought a dog home that someone had given him one day. I'm not sure what breed it was, but the dog was angry and violent all the time. He bit several of my siblings, but my father kept him in the house with us. Why would a man keep a dog that bites his children? I have often asked myself that question. We were so afraid of him and scared to make any fast moves. The dog only loved my father. So finally one day we let him out of the house, and he never came back. That was one of the happiest days of my life. We were just as afraid of him as we were my father; the very sound of his voice scared me so bad until I could barely speak. His presence just brought a dark cloud all around the house.

We could never entertain friends when he was home for fear that a fight would break out. He didn't want us to participate in activities outside of the home; his slogan was "There are enough of you all to play with each other." Can you imagine

being so afraid that you couldn't eat, reluctant to talk, and

scared to close your eyes to sleep for fear? My mother's voice

crying and begging him not to hit her just because he could do

so caused so much fear to take root in my heart.

I read a book that said violence against women impacts

everyone, especially girls as well as the health and wellness of

the family as a whole. I can agree with that statement because

each of my siblings has some type of dysfunctional behavior.

Several are afraid of love and commitment, and they have

never been married. Some are working all the time and don't

have enough time for family. There is one in particular whom I

fear has a severe case of anger and resentment, but refuses any type of help because of denial. It's sad when you think that you are normal, but everyone around you knows that something is wrong.

When my mother finally decided to divorce my father, all of the damage had been done. She filed the papers without my father's knowledge. We were all still living under the same roof. He was reading the paper one Saturday morning and came across the divorce column. I heard him yell out and began to cry. His footsteps walking toward my bedroom sounded so loudly in my ear. My heart pounded so fast because I didn't know what he was about to do. I was still in bed with the bedroom door open as he stood in the hallway and looked into my eyes. With tears in his eyes as if he was in pain, he said to me, "Angie, your mother is divorcing me." I looked into his eyes and felt nothing. I pulled the covers over my face and began to pray. He voiced demeaning words and statements at me and my mother. They were the ugliest words a being could speak.

He left the house, and it gave me some relief. I knew he would be back with a vengeance. He had to go and get his whiskey in order to play out his role. After the divorce, my mother took ownership of the house, but my father kept coming back saying, "I paid the cost to be the boss." He said that the house was his because he had paid for it. One night as we slept in our beds, he broke down the front door and came in. He began to terrorize the entire house. My mother did nothing, just allowed him to scare all of us. What could she do? She was just as afraid, but God kept all of us from harm. He wouldn't stop harassing us. It was as if the divorce had never taken place.

I recall watching a television show named *The Burning Bed* and some of the same events that took place in the picture also took place in my parent's home. The woman was being degraded for the way she looked or if she looked too long at one of her husband's friends. Her mother said that he was just a little jealous and that it's normal for a man to be that way. She also told her to stand by her man because a woman needs a husband. I saw my mother mistreated in the same manner. She went to work daily with black eyes, bruised arms, and a wrecked body full of pain. The man in the film was so terrible, his own parents were afraid of him. The woman had divorced him and told him to get out of her life. The laws were painfully unfair. If the authorities didn't see the act of abuse happen, then there was nothing they could do.

One evening we were all watching TV, and my father broke into my mother's house again. He was intoxicated as usual and began to threaten me. I was sitting in a chair, and he put his finger in my face. I snatched my head away from him, and he lifted the chair from the floor and flipped it over on top of me. I was two months pregnant at the time. No one has the right to use violence in order to solve any problems, whether it is mother, father or husband. I asked why did I have such an awful father, and the voice of God said, "You are my child. I will protect and keep you."

The experiences that I went through were a training camp for issues yet to come. I would be well equipped to handle the people that I would meet along my way, I thought. I dreamed of having my own family one day that included a husband and two children. The man that I married was a dreamer too, but soon those dreams became a nightmare. He never went to church but in the beginning of our relationship professed to be in church. He said that he understood that being in a covenant with God was the only way to live. When I accepted his hand in marriage it gave me a false sense of security. I cried until I didn't have tears left in my eyes. My whole life flashed before me. I was only twenty years old when I married because I was intrigued with what he could do for me. I wanted to leave my father's house and get away from the abuse. The husband was my ticket out, but I didn't know the price that I had to pay. How can you share a home, the same bed, food and children with someone that you don't even know? Some people get married for all the wrong reasons. I was one of those people. Marriage is a covenant that includes three (a man, woman, and Christ our Lord). When you don't invite Christ to the wedding, then the marriage will not last. The pastor would speak these words, and I thought that I understood them. But what I didn't realize is that God had not blessed this union because it was not in His will. He placed that man in my life for a reason, but it was not for marriage.

Sometimes people come into our life for a reason: to teach a lesson that we so desperately need. Often, when it's time for them to leave we hold on to them so tight because we have not learned our lesson. Looking back I have a lot of regrets. Why couldn't I see the writing on the wall? He was my escape from the mistreatment that I feared daily. Yet he was cold, calculating, and trusted know one. The definition of disrespectful, angry, and negative words were tattooed across his forehead. My mother asked me why did I get married so young, and I told her that I just wanted to leave home. She did not respond. I wanted to get as far away from her and my father as I possibly could. Little did I know that I would endure some of the same treatment I'd so desperately attempted to escape.

Chapter Ten

I was always afraid to speak because of the lashing that I would receive. She has never apologized for her actions because she doesn't feel that she did anything wrong. I blamed my parents for a lot of things over the years, but I have come to realize that the emotional ups and downs I went through were supposed to happen to me in order for me to build my faith with the Holy Spirit. He brought me through the confusion and acts of violence in order for me to grow and trust in Him. I have traveled a long, hard road. Several times I thought that I

was by myself, but God assured me that He has been with me

and is still with me. My parents wanted me to stay a child

forever so that they would have the control. I never understood

that until now. My father wanted to be in control and keep me

bound and begging to him for all of my needs.

When I was getting ready to graduate from high school I told

my parents that I wanted to go to college and they both said,

"No." I was a slave in my own home. Cooking, cleaning, and

taking care of my siblings was my calling. The only thing I

learned is that I'm supposed to take care of others. I took on

the burdens of trying to solve all my family's problems. They

came to me for the answers and now some of them resent me

for helping them. I put them all first in my life even after my

marriage. After the marriage ended, I became very depressed,

but I didn't know how depressed. Some days I couldn't get out

of bed. I acted out just like my mother. I mistreated my

children and nobody understood the pain and anguish that I

suffered. I did not like myself and the misery that I put others

through. I thought if I had gone off to college or moved to

another town where nobody knew me then things would have

been different. The shame of it all just mortified me to tears

day after endless day. I tried to start drinking on a regular

basis, but that didn't work. I fell into a sea of dating men that

was not my type, and Lord only knows the madness that went

along with it. I would befriend all of the wrong people, men and women. I started hanging out in night clubs and waking

the next morning and not knowing how I got home. I was in

and out of the emergency room basically just to get attention. I

wanted someone to feel sorry for me and to take on my

responsibilities. I didn't want to care for my children because I

felt that they deserved a better mother. How could I be a

mother with the worst training that I can describe? I wanted

the doctor to find something wrong with me and to just put me

into a padded room and that way I wouldn't have to deal with

anything. My children stayed with family members most of the

time. I can't tell you the state that I was in not knowing how

we were going to make ends meet. I was uneducated,

untrained, and mentally drained to even know how to pick up

the pieces. In the meantime, one of my brothers attending

college became very ill. His becoming sick saved me from all

the heartache that I was going through. It gave me time to

transform all my energy into what was happening to him;

therefore I didn't have time to think about my problems. He

needed a liver transplant. If he didn't receive it in a hurry, then

he was going to pass away. He was placed on a waiting list at

a care facility. At that time I was still living in my hometown,

but I kept in close contact with him. He would call me when

he wanted to come home and visit.

Chapter Eleven

Finally, the Lord spoke to my heart and said "Go to Nashville".

I picked up my kids and off we went on a mission without a

plan. I had no money, no job, not even a place to live, but I

had faith in God. I didn't have transportation to get there

because the same sibling had wrecked my car earlier that year.

I met a man through some friends, and he liked me very much.

He wanted to help me, my son, and daughter. When we got to

the city, I began the journey of mother, nurse, and live-in maid.

I was so alone with the numerous decisions that had to be

made. The administrator at the hospital had given me a beeper

and told me that when it goes off to get to the care center as

soon as possible. He had developed jaundice and his eyes were

as yellow as the sun. His weight changed frequently and his

facial make-up was almost unidentifiable. When he was as close to meeting his maker as one can get, the pager finally went off. They had a donor. He was scared and confused, but I comforted him as much as I could. He underwent seven hours of surgery. The jaundice stayed with him for a while and his eyes were still yellow. He always wore a disguise to cover his eyes. He even instructed the surgeon to put sunglasses on after his surgery was over. I would pray for him day in and day out, and afterwards I would tell him to pray for himself. He was released from the hospital five days after the surgery and sent home to me. He had to take about 25 types of prescription meds. The nurse made a color coded chart with the names of each drug and how much to take at what time. He laid in his bed filled with pain and whispered to me that he

wished he was dead. He was only twenty-four years old. As a

senior in college and in the prime of his life, he should have

been up and about going to basketball games, participating in

homecoming activities, and dating. He was a young man with

talent, and art was his hobby. He was honored one year for

painting a mural in one of the elementary schools here in the

city. I bathed him like he was my son and put food into his

mouth. I pushed the medications in his mouth when he didn't

even want to take them. He wanted to give up, but I wouldn't

let him. I was just as scared as he was because I thought that I

might do something wrong and make him sick. I had to take

care of him and two little ones of my own. I had to focus most of my attention on my patient which made others become

second, and I'm sure they didn't like that. Sometimes I try to

speak to them about the things that took place in our

household, and my daughter just says, "I don't remember that."

It makes me feel good that she doesn't remember because I

know that she is being honest. If my son or daughter was given

a certain amount of time to live or needed a major organ, there

is no way that I would be living in another city waiting to see

what happens. I would pack my bags and come to my

children's bedside to let them know just how much I love them.

The staff often asked, "Where is his mother?" I made up

excuses for her, but I don't know where her mental state was at

that time. She just checked out as usual and left me holding the bag. It's like nothing moves her. She doesn't share her

emotions and very seldom shares any secrets. I try to talk to

my mother about the experiences and when I mention it, her

reply would be "I don't remember." Well, I don't believe her.

I have often asked her about seeing a counselor, but she said

that she doesn't believe in psychiatry. She keeps her feelings

hidden inside, yet sometimes it comes out in anger. She is very

bitter, and the older she gets, the harder it is for me to

communicate with her at all. I love my mother, but I will not

take any more abuse or angry words. The Bible states that it's

okay to get angry, but sin not. It states that you should get

angry at the right things. Cruel treatment is never okay, and it

often leaves a bitter taste in my mouth. It gives you a phobia and makes you fearful to trust and disables you to love.

Everything that I did for my brother was out of love. After he

got well enough to go back to school and I found my own

apartment, it was time for me to start a new job. His body was

healed, but his mind needed another type of healing. I wonder

how he thinks or feel about our mother. Does he ask the same

questions: Why didn't she come to his aide when he needed

her, and why did she just allow me to take over? I had a

conversation with my mother about the caretakers at the

hospital, and it caused her to become upset. Angrily she said,

"Don't they know that I have a job. I can't just leave my job."

I would explain to them that she lived in another city and

couldn't get away because of her job. In my opinion, that was just an excuse not to participant in her son's care. They looked

at me as if I was crazy. "I can't get away because of my job" I

heard them say in my mind. Doesn't she know that her son is

facing terminal illness? Someone has to pass away before her

son can even live. She may not have the chance to speak to

him ever again, and she is worried about her job. These were

the thoughts going through my head, but I never repeated it.

We could barely get by some days, but there was no one to call

on but God. They all just allowed me to take on the

responsibility. It just makes me feel that the selfishness that

my father taught through his actions had rubbed off on my

siblings. I don't blame them for their shortcomings, but I need

all of them to make a change. I want them to recognize that we were all mistreated, and it made each of us who we are today.

We are living our lives trying not to remember the pain and

torture, but we all need to be healed, both mind and spirit.

Chapter Twelve

As life went on, I was introduced to a young man who worked

in my office. He was tall in stature, thin, and very good

looking. On the day we met, I was delivering paperwork to the

payroll department, and I didn't know exactly where to go. He

and a few other guys were sitting in the lobby. I heard my

name being called, and I walked over toward them. I

recognized one of the men, and he introduced me to this tall

male better known as Bobby. I told him that I was looking for

the payroll department and this individual standing over six feet tall volunteered to show me to the elevator and then proceeded to ride with me to the third floor. I thought to myself, "He is very tall and good looking. I'm sure he is not available." I found out later that he was unattached, and I should have asked Why? A few weeks had gone by, and my life was upside down. Bobby started sending me love notes through a fellow co-worker. I guess he didn't make a very good impression on me because I couldn't remember his face. The co-worker tried to describe him, but it didn't jar my memory. I asked her to walk over to the building with me so that I could get another look at him. When she and I got to his office, he was standing in the doorway. She said, "There he is. That's Bobby." I said, "Are you the one sending the notes? And he responded, "Yes, are you disappointed?" I replied, "No, I'm not" and gave him my telephone number. The day I gave him my telephone number placed me on a roller coaster ride that I'm still on. At first, he called and called, but I was very reluctant to speak to him. I was not getting the right vibes, and I had not prayed for a relationship. I would get into my car and drive to my hometown every weekend. Months had passed by, and he was still calling. Finally I allowed him to take me to dinner, and during our lengthy conversation, the subject of marriage came up. He asked me how long would we have to date before marriage. I thought it was a strange topic of conversation, but I did respond by saying that I would need to get to know the man before I could make him my husband. It was a very serious subject on his part, but I didn't take it so seriously. Marriage (yea, right) is what I thought. He was so proud and happy to have me in his life. He wanted all of his friends and family members to meet me. We moved too fast, making all of the wrong decisions. He was so protective of me. It was as if he wanted to shield me from all my hurt and pain.

I felt a strong connection between us, and it often left me speechless when we were together. I had a lot of baggage with me: personal issues resulting from a broken home, a failed marriage and two teenagers. He had never been married. However, he could relate to coming from a broken home because he was in the same boat. The only difference was that his family was not that close, and his mother was deceased. He understood my pain or dealt with it as much as he could. I was very fragile, and I had many secrets. I wasn't about to let him into my space because I didn't feel that he was worthy. I prayed to God to help me with my feelings and to fix all of this man's issues if he was meant to be with me. I once took him home to Memphis for the annual celebration. We watched a free concert on the river. My mother, Bobby, and I went to have some fun, but it soon took a turn for the worse. As soon as the concert started, Bobby had had several beers and was overly aggressive. He got into an argument with some men who made a statement that just ticked him off. My mother looked at me and said that I would never be able to control that temper. On another occasion, we went out to a night club. Bobby got intoxicated to the point that he had to be carried out to the car. I was the designated driver, and when I pulled up to his parent's house, he had fallen asleep. I touched him to wake him up and he began taking off his clothes and cursing so loudly that he woke up the neighbors. I was really embarrassed by the whole ordeal. The next morning I managed to get home without his knowledge, and he called me later that evening using a very bitter tone to let me know that he didn't appreciate my leaving without his knowledge. We were just dating or trying to get to know each other. You would think that I would have stopped seeing him, but I didn't. After he sobered up, he was very apologetic. I asked him to stop calling, but he didn't.

Family members who knew him would say all he needs is a good woman in his life. I am a good woman, spirit filled, steadfast and unmovable in my faith, but I knew that I couldn't change him or control him. I received a job transfer to another city and I thought this is my ticket out of the relationship. I didn't have the heart to tell him that he just wasn't for me, so I told him that I had to go home to my teenagers, who at the time were living with their father. When Bobby and I said our goodbyes, tears fell from his eyes, and it melted my heart. I left the town that had been my home for the last five years, but I told him that we could keep in touch. We talked everyday, and on each passing day I realized that he didn't have a clue about being in a relationship with God. He had no vision about the future or any goals. He was just surviving from day to day.

Chapter Thirteen

He was not husband or father material. Knowing this only made me work harder to achieve the things that I wanted for myself. At first, I thought that I had to have a man in my world in order to have success. I finally realized that I'm perfectly made by the Creator. I have a mind that functions in proper order and all of my body parts operate like a well-oiled machine. I can achieve whatever I set my mind to through our Lord and Savior who strengthens me. Looking back in time I wasn't living that way at all. When I prayed and asked God to fix my situation, I didn't leave it up to Him. I tried to help Him along the way. I had seen the worst side of Bobby, and I decided to send him a letter. In my letter, I described the life that I wanted and the things that I didn't want him doing. I talked about his friends, our finances, and Christ being the head of our household. He was very agreeable with me on each subject and would attend church with me whenever he came to visit. He even got to the point where he was going to church each Sunday mornings alone and had started asking his family to go with him. I saw something in him that I wanted so badly that I overlooked his faults, which were many. After being in the relationship for about two years, our company had a very lavish Christmas party. I was still working in the office back home. I came to the party in Nashville, and Bobby surprised me with an engagement ring. I accepted it, and we started planning our wedding. How could I do this again? Marriage is such a big step, and it takes courage to give someone your heart. I did not understand God's plan at this time and I didn't know how it was all going to unfold. After our wedding, my father became very sick. He had gone blind several years before and needed help but refused due to his pride. This time he'd had a stroke and was paralyzed. I would take him back and forward to his appointments and Bobby would assist me. I had to arrange for him to go into a rehabilitation center and he was not pleased. On the day that he was to leave the center, I asked for spiritual guidance to tell my father that he had to go into the nursing home. A minister met me at the care center to explained to him how ill he was and that he couldn't possibly go home after his rehabilitation treatment. He nodded as if he understood the magnitude of his illness. Then she prayed with my father and shook his hand. After she left the hospital room he totally went off on me. His abusive words returned flowing just like they did when I was a child. He used harsh profanity as if he was talking to a stranger on the street. He degraded me and yelled to high heavens about the way I was handling his care. He said that he wanted to go home, and I refused to allow that nonsense. The medics came and took him to the rehabilitation center and my father fought me daily on his having to stay there. I bought all of his clothes and personal items that he needed. I took snacks and goodies for his

enjoyment. I went to the center weekly to take care of washing

his clothes and to make sure that he wasn't being mistreated. I

brought him the special things that he liked hoping some life

pleasures would calm his spirit. Isn't that funny? I felt that I

owed him something. I would sit and visit to share my stories

with him, but he wasn't satisfied. He didn't have his beer and

cigarettes to share in his sorrow. I didn't share with anyone the

problems that I was having with my father, but he was a real

pain. He would tell the administrator of the facility that he

wanted to go home, and she would call me at my job telling me

to come and get him. I told her that he had no one to care for

him at home. She said that was not her problem and that she

wouldn't be able to house him against his will. One night as I

was preparing to go to an event, there was a knock at my front

door. It was my father's siblings asking for help. I allowed them in and awaited to hear what they had to say. "Come and go with us to speak to your father," they said. I complied with their request, and they vowed that they would stand by the decision that I had made for his care. When I arrived at the center, my father was sitting in his wheelchair waiting for me. We gathered in the conference room to discuss the matter of him leaving. The administrator gave us a few minutes alone and said that she would be back for our decision. A statement was made that we would have my father put into a mental institution if he didn't comply with my wishes. My father agreed that he would stay in the rehabilitation center until he regained his ability to walk. Several months went by, and he did regain the use of his legs. After he left the center, we stopped speaking to each other for a while, and I didn't know that he had gotten sick again. This time it was very serious, and he was in a life threatening situation. He had developed gangrene in both of his feet. I was still living in town, and Bobby was in his own world holding down the fort. He would travel back and forth to spend time with me and the kids. I was spending a lot of time taking care of my father. The doctor said that my father was too weak to operate on, and if he regained strength, he would have to have both feet amputated. The doctor also said that he wouldn't allow my father to go back home, meaning he would have to spend the remaining years in a nursing home. I spent most mornings before work going to the care facility to feed him. I used my lunch hour to take care of his personal business and after work, I took care of both him and my family. I have many siblings, and not one lifted a finger to even give him a cup of water. I was so tired, but I never complained. I asked one of my siblings to take my father something to eat one day. Though she didn't want to do it, my father did inform me later that she brought him a hamburger. Depressed and speechless, my father laid in his bed. His frail body was filled with pain. He was angrier now than before. I heard him cursing out one of the caretakers as I approached his room one day. I told her that I was sorry for his actions, and she said that it was okay. It takes a strong caregiver to take care of the evil ones. One of my siblings came to visit and asked my father if he was ready to go to heaven. My father replied nodding yes with his head. He didn't know who we were at times. I felt sorry for my father and the suffering that he was going through, but I had not forgotten the pain that he put me through all of my years. My heart was filled with grief even before he passed away. It was about 3:00 a.m. in the morning when my phone rang. I was in bed asleep and as I answered the phone, a voice said that my father's condition had changed and that I needed to come to the care facility immediately. I stopped at my mother's house and picked her up. When we arrived at our destination, we were

met by the chaplain. He explained that my father was having

trouble breathing and that I would not have wanted him to

continue living in such distress. He said that my father

struggled even as he took his final breath. I began to cry in my

mother's arms, but I just wanted to lose control and scream,

"He's gone. Thank God he's gone." The doctor asked if I

wanted to see him, and I said, "Yes." I went into his cold room

where he laid lifeless. I was in shock and relieved all at the

same time. I whispered, "Good-bye Daddy" as I kissed him on

his forehead. This was the only time that a spirit of peace

came over me in the presence of my father. I felt calm and

secure in knowing that he could not hurt me again. The

thought that I am surely safe finally hit me. I never felt safe

with him, and I was so afraid of his actions over the years that it left me with an inability to give my heart to anyone that crossed my path.

Chapter fourteen

A person is suppose to feel safe in a home with parents more so than any place in this world. This man that I called father was finally only a memory. His ugly words, disrespectful actions, uncaring and unfeeling ways were now all gone. His demise affected each of my siblings individually, but collectively we shared the same pain. My heart was broken, and my thoughts were that I never got to share with him like a daughter shares with her father. I didn't learn anything from him except how to fight. I will never know if he loved me. I will never understand the true meaning of a father's love. I heard the preacher say that a daughter should not accept a man that does not have the standards of her father. A real father sets the stage for his daughter and molds her into a dignified young lady that has self-respect. He spoils her with gifts and compliments. He disciplines according to the word of God for it is written that a father should not provoke his children, but bring them up in a Godly manner that they shall never forget. She will never detour from her father's teachings, and she will find a man that has the same standards he upheld. My father took the love that I gave him, and he stomped it in the ground every day. He terrified me so badly that it hindered me from loving others. I regret that more than any teachings that I have ever learned. I would try to be different with my children by giving them love and praising for their achievements. I think of how my son and daughter would never know the love of a grandfather. They would never have a grandfather like I had growing up, a man that was filled with agape love. He had only positive and precious words that flowed from his mouth. He would give you the shirt off of his back in the name of love. I once told my father that I wished he was dead long before it happened, and when it became a reality, my heart broke into a million pieces. I had to make seven phone calls to my siblings and what a challenging ordeal that turned out to be. It was still early in the morning and the chaplain held my hand and walked me through those calls. I called my oldest sibling first, and finally got a voice on the phone. I started to give the same scenario as the chaplain gave to me about how impossible it was for our father to breathe. When I finished the news all of their responses were the same: I'll get home as soon as I can. No yelling, screaming or outburst. It was only calm reactions. The next call was made and so on and on. I called many other family members and to my surprise they were very upset. Some we knew, and some we didn't. My father had a very large family, but they all had their problems. It seemed that we never saw each other unless someone was laying in front of the church alter. Why would you want to go to a funeral to see the remains of your beloved family member whom you have not spoken to in years? Is it too late or is that the only way to face them? We all came together and planned a memorial that was very tasteful and graceful. It was out of the normal of how my father lived, but as they say the funeral is for the living. All of my friends were there to console me with their unconditional love. None of them knew the terrible experiences that I suffered under my father's leadership. I have never described in detail how inhumane the words that I grew up with affected me. No one knows the trouble I've seen accept God Almighty. My father was buried in a veterans' cemetery, but sometimes I feel his ghost still lives on in some of my siblings. There are several who are bitter and evil flows daily. Some are broken in spirit and try to hide their pain. They can't hide it from me, because I see it every time I visit. I hear it in their voices when I speak to them on the phone. My father really did a number on all of us, but we are all saved by grace. I can accept the statement that I heard a man say, that as kids we praise our parents, but when we grow up, we judge them. I'm not the judge over my parents, because we all will have a judgment day. I just know now that the way we lived was wrong. If I had the chance to write him a letter, it would read something like this:

Dear Daddy,

I was hurt and disappointed at the harsh treatment that you gave me. I often thought that it was my fault for the way you acted toward me. Maybe it was something I said or something I did. I don't think that I ever did anything to please you. You never gave me a kind word or a loving hand. You wore the face of evil both day and night. I

never felt protected, special or wanted by you. I was

nervous, frightened, and speechless more often than I can

remember. I disliked you for making me feel all of these

things at such a young age. I didn't see my life unfolding in

the manner that it did and I used to blame you for

everything that went wrong. Now, I realize that I had the

power to stop allowing you to hurt me, but I didn't use it.

You were not the father that I deserved, but you're the one

that I got. I forgive you for all the bad days and I applaud

you for the good because I'm sure there were some good

days.

Sincerely,

Angie

P.S. I love you

Chapter fifteen

I see that the bitterness that I have inside still eats at me. I try to control it by hiding my true feelings, but I can't. I have lost jobs and friends because of it. I blame others for my faults and my shortcomings. I pray for forgiveness, but it's so hard for me to forgive others. The people that I'm referring to are my closest relatives, friends and mother. Some of these people have come and gone. I know that people come into your life for a reason or a season, but I have always tried to keep everyone close to me. I can't share my true identity with anyone. I'm like a tailored suit that was put together wrong. One sleeve is longer than the other, so I tuck the sleeve under to make it the same length as my arm. The pants' seat hang too low, and I use pins to fix it. Both of the legs are too long, but I wear 3 inch heels so it won't drag. This describes my life, and how I try to live without anyone knowing the truth. What is the truth? I have a pretty face that is all made up with beautifully colored make-up, and everywhere I go people tell me how pretty I am. When

I look into the mirror, all I see is the pain that I hold deep within. It's

so deep that my heart hurts when I remember some of the cruelty that

has haunted me most of my days. I have been told that I have low

self-esteem, and I'm co-dependent. These words carry a lot of weight

and describe so many people. It has never been my desire to be

anything other than an independent woman with goals and a

successful positive outlook. I went back to work, and my husband

was still living in the city where we met. He was no help in my time

of darkness. He drank more and more and was so intoxicated at the

funeral services that I just cried for him. After things slowed down a

bit, we decided that I would leave my job and move back to

Nashville. I really didn't have time to grieve. I saw a friend at

church one Sunday afternoon, and he asked if I was losing weight? I

went home and looked into the mirror and sure enough my clothes

were falling off of me. I went to the doctor and my weight had dropped to about 80 pounds. When I got home to my husband I thought to myself my troubles are now over, but they were not over yet. Instead they were just beginning. How could I know what the Lord was doing in my home when all I saw weekend after weekend was drunken gatherings of Bobby's friends? I witnessed men and women parading back and forth partying while drinking beer and whiskey in my family room. I listened to angry, nasty name calling and violence in my bedroom. One night I was babysitting two of my nephews and one of them told me that it was his birthday. I decided to take them to the mall and buy a birthday gift. We went to the Disney store, and I allowed each one of them to pick out a toy. After we paid for the items, I said that it was time to go home. I arrived on my street, and I saw all of these cars parked in front of my house. I thought to myself, *"Someone must be having a party."* Little did I know that the party was at my home! I walked into the house and told the boys to go to their bedrooms. When I made it to the top of the staircase I could hear the music playing very loudly. I went downstairs to see what was going on in my home, and to my surprise three ladies were sitting in my den. My husband met me with the biggest smile and said, "Baby let me introduce you." His friend, partner in crime, replied, "I will introduce the ladies." He began to name each one and told them my name. They didn't even respond. Not a single word came out of their mouths, and I was in shock. I asked Bobby to come upstairs, and I informed him that everyone had to vacant the premises right then. He was so upset about it and told me that I wasn't being fair. I told him that the whole setup was very disrespectful and that he does not give social gatherings of that nature without me. He didn't see anything wrong with it because his friend called and asked if he could bring the ladies over. I was offended that he would think that the situation would be okay with me. Year after year I put up with the friends and their foolishness. I have often left home like my mother used to do, thinking that if I left then he will wake up and see that things have got to change. The neighbors were offended and disgusted by the unruly events that took place at my address. I have had several complaints from them regarding my husband and his friends' loud noise. The friends have no respect for anyone, not even their own parents. They used words that cut like a knife and are hardly ever forgotten. You can break a person's spirit by what comes out of your mouth. I was feeling trapped in my marriage like a caged animal. There would be arguments before we went to work and after I returned from work. He had road rage and no patience for his fellow man. He drove too fast when he was angry and it truly terrified me. I spent a week in a hotel trying to think of a way out. I went to work everyday as if nothing was wrong, and finally I couldn't take it anymore. I quite my job and wanted to check into a mental hospital until the Lord revealed to me just how to handle my marriage. I could hear Bobby begging and pleading in my sleep for me to come home, but I was on God's time. He always lied and said that he would do better, but just after a week or so he would

be back in the same routine. It was a very devastating period in my

life because it kept me on the defense. I tried to shield my kids from

a lot of the negative forces that we faced from day to day. Then

suddenly we would have unexpected house guests. On a daily basis

my house became the hangout for unruly guest. I wouldn't allow

anyone to come in especially if my husband wasn't home. My

grandmother taught me to present myself as a lady at all times and in

every situation. Men coming to and from my home were not a sign of

a righteous woman living behind these walls.

Chapter sixteen

Confusion and chaos were present on every hand. Later that

day, I sent my daughter to live with one of my brothers. Why

should my daughter have to leave her home? My husband in a

effort to solve some of our issues only made it worst by using a lot of profanity. Who could live like this? I went to church on Sunday mornings, and I would just cry. I had prayer partners and I would call them in the middle of the night, but I couldn't see the resolution. The years had gone by so fast. When I looked up, I had been married for five years. We didn't celebrate anything in my house. I would try to have a Happy Thanksgiving, a Merry Christmas, and a Happy New Year, but the whole day would be like a dream that I could not awake from no matter how much I desperately tried. My body and mind were taken over by a woman that just stood still and watched in shock at the drinking and violence that transpired throughout the day. The same situation that I grew up in came back from the grave. I used to have nightmares of my father rising up from his casket speaking angry words at me. Many times I thought that I was being punished for all of the wrong I had done. I came to realize that it was a test, a test of my faith and trust that God would protect me and provide all of my needs. The pressures from each event had taken over my mind, and I was trapped in a world of insane people whom had not been diagnosed. I thought to myself if my father was so angry and abusive to me, then what happened in Bobby's up-bringing to make him that way. Bobby had already given me a brief history of what went on in his childhood. We tell stories about what happened in our homes, and it all seem so unreal. People say, "You need to get over it." But how do you do that when each day of your decision making is influenced by the way you were raised. Each time I saw my parents argue or fight, it showed me how to treat my mate. Also, with parenting my own, it prepared me on how to discipline. Once I was combing my daughter's hair and reprimanding her for something that she had done. All of a sudden, she fainted in my arms and it scared me so badly until I began to change my tone whenever I punished her and my son. I tried very hard not to treat them in the same manner that my parents treated me, but it was very hard. When you are used to doing something wrong all of the time, change is very difficult to get use too. I prayed a lot and put them into positive circles. I trained them to have morals and to be respectful around their elders. You can tell when a person has been taught old-school manners or hasn't been taught manners at all. Looking back, I think it was very hard on the two of them when I married Bobby. Though they have always respected him, they have never thought of him as a father figure. Honestly, he never acted like a father in our home, only a little boy who needed a father. He was very cold at times, and the things that he did were over the edge. I wondered if he had a soul or a heart. His actions were heartless. He had a dark side to him, but I understand that he was hiding behind the hurt and anger that controlled his emotions. Confusion and misunderstanding lead the mornings and throughout the night. How could you love someone and hurt them all at the same time? I planned a moving party with my friends and moved most of the furniture to storage and checked into a motel. I was always on the same roller coaster again and again moving from place to place. I was so destroyed and depressed about the whole ordeal until I could not function. I was always running away. That was me. Bobby said that he was sorry and didn't mean to hurt me and wanted me to come home. I didn't feel completely comfortable about coming home with our guest still sharing the house with us. Reluctantly, I moved back home and things truly did get better. This was due to the fact that we finally had the house to ourselves since our houseguest had departed. He moved into his own apartment houseguest and God only knows what all went on in that home. There were drug dealings, parties every weekend, and some of the most disgusting events that I have ever witness, and believe me. I've seen a lot. All of his friends were either using drugs or selling drugs. Or they were homeless or jobless due to drug use and abuse. I had a sincere passion to save him from his addictions, but I didn't know how. Once again our world was turned upside down, but this time God stepped in. My husband suffered a terrible loss when his loved one passed away. His was a life ended too soon without a signal or a sign. He had been sick, but no one knew why or how long. The people he trusted and the women he shared with all took a negative toll on his health. The day my husband came home and I looked into his eyes, I saw a scared little boy filled with anger and resentment. He gave me a hug and said that he was glad to see me. I told him that I was happy to see him as well, but it was just untrue. I knew that pain would soon find its way into our hearts. After he moved out and began working on a steady job, I knew something had changed within him. Driving the hotel van, picking up passengers from the airport had made him into a new man. Then and only then, I began to exhale and breathe again. I also thought long and hard about the type of job that he had. Can you imagine this intoxicated soul driving all those people to and fro? The trusting people didn't know the danger that their lives were in. I deeply think about it now more often when I'm boarding an airplane or getting a shuttle bus to my hotel. This world is filled with people who are addicted to something or someone. Finally God said, "Enough is enough." He knew how tired we all were. God took him home to rest, but it wasn't easy for Bobby to live with that fact. He went through sleepless nights, and he would awake crying from his sleep. He made all kind of crazy decisions that affected our household. He stopped working and depended solely on me. I would come home and find him sitting in the dark. He cut off some friends and family members by not accepting phone calls. This went on far too long. He woke up one morning and told me that he was going to drive his truck into the river and I felt every part of his pain because at one point, I wanted to do the same. But, I know a man named Jesus who can fix any man or problem if we just give it to Him. I was so sick of his drama that I told him to do whatever would make him happy. I got dressed and got in my car and drove away. It was time to let God be God. I had no control over him or his actions. I had had enough of his foolish ways. I asked God that if Bobby did drive off into the river that He would allow me to keep my sanity and be able to live without him. I decided to speak to him about his actions, and it only angered him. He told me to get out and never come back. I left the house for a while, but I did come back. He has shut me out more times than I can remember with name calling and physical confrontation. He never remembered any of his actions. It was if he blacked out or something. He remembers what he wants to remember. He remembers a wedding day and words spoken. "For better or worse, in sickness and good health, until my dying day, I will always love you." He reminds me of those words when he feels that I'm mistreating him. Last year I went to see a counselor and I told her about some of the terrible things that had happened in my home. She said that God gives us the answers to our prayers, but we chose not to hear Him. She explained that several, earlier events that had occurred were moments of opportunity to exit my marriage. She also said that I married my father. I didn't agree with her at that time, and I became angry and resentful. Why would I marry someone exactly like my father?

Chapter seventeen

Thinking back when Bobby and my father first met, there was an instant bond between them. It was unspoken, but it happened because Bobby was always there to help me with my father's needs. As a matter of fact, we were planning to bring my father to our home to live with us before he got terminally ill. There are a lot of things that I don't know about my father, and I'm sure that I will never know. There are skeletons in my husband's past that he has not shared with me and maybe they are so devastating that I wouldn't be able to handle them, but whatever they are, they're not allowing him to lead a healthy life. He is just existing on a daily basis without any vision or focus. Why did I come back just to receive more pain over and over again? He began to drink and use drugs more and more as the years went by. Many times he tried to stop, but he never gave up the friends that were doing the same thing. He didn't want to live and I know why. He was overcome with grief and guilt. He wouldn't confront his selfish pride and acknowledge his self inflicted circumstances. The voice of God was calling him and still is, but he won't let go of his pride. He refuses to let the negative friends and family members go. These are the same people who laugh at him and insult him behind his back. He won't consider the possibility of new surroundings, without the same faces who are holding him back. He can't envision a spiritual life with God showing him that he is the head and not the tail. My prayer is that he finds the courage to walk away from it all and find his Father who is in heaven. I stay awake most nights praying and wondering why did God give this man to me, but I realize that he didn't give him to me. I just accepted him and God had nothing to do with it. The mental suffering alone could have sent me to my grave but God said, "no, you are mine." I count it all joy, the things that have happened to me, because I'm still living and sharing. When I was going through the scenarios I couldn't find the joy that I have in my heart now, but I have come to realize that there were many lessons that I was suppose to learn. The lesson that I learned from my grandparents was that I have to have a prayer life in order to function day to day. They also taught me how to love unconditionally. I really can't say that I would not have tried to end my existence if I didn't have my grandparents. The thought came to my mind on many occasions because of the events that took place in my father's house. My parents taught me that you don't have to mistreat others in order to survive. Treating others with a harsh word is never the answer. It is never okay to hurt the ones that you love. I learned that abusive behavior is not brought on by alcohol or drugs but by a lack of love. If a person is cold and unfeeling that's because love was never taught. My husband taught me not to put my trust in man, but that all my trust

belongs to God.   Through our marriage I also learned how to

forgive. I pray for the people who have come and gone in my

world. My past still remain a problem for me, but I hold on to

my joy. I don't allow anyone to steal my joy. In any battle,

you must know your enemy. People will try to destroy you,

but you can't run from God. The Lord will deliver you from

all evil works and preserve you for growth. I have moved on

and forgiven each one for all of their ugly tricks. I can recall

the night that a voice from the past called me. I could hear the

pain in his speech as he asked for my forgiveness. My heart

went out to him for just making the effort.   It has taken me

several years to forgive many people in my life's journey, and

even at the age of fifty I'm still finding out that I had some

unforgiveness in my heart. Bobby, my beloved, has shown me

that people can change if they want too. Change is a scary and powerful thing, but sometimes is necessary in order to survive.

I don't blame the past or present for the pain that I have

received. Their families taught them that it was okay to be that

way. However it was their responsibility to change and not

give in to the generational curse that was placed upon them.

After all, we are all human and none are perfect. We misspeak.

We forget. We buy when we should sell. We miss

opportunities, and we are sometimes blind to the obvious. My

mother, for instance, was born in a loving and spirit filled

home, but she chose a man filled with an inability to love.

There were never any teachings about God in my father's

house. The two of them came together and instead of finding

love, kindness and companionship, they found only heartache.

Out of their heartache, seven beautiful children were born.

They deserved a father and mother to give them security and a

strong start to be prepared for this world. As a matter of fact that's what everyone deserves. Strong character building comes from strong parents that is committed to something other than self.

Chapter eighteen

Marriage and parenthood is not for the weak, selfish, confused, or prideful man. Therefore, if you came from a past characterized by any of those things, it is your responsibility to get yourself in order before inviting anyone else into your circle. I remember going to a therapist because of a relationship that I was in and it was not going well. The therapist told me that I was in the relationship because I was looking for a father figure. I couldn't accept that then, but I have come to realize that it was true. My father was in the household with me, but he was never a father. This family only knew how to solve their problems through violence. I couldn't get away from the cruelty no matter how hard I tried. I have to consider that my world has only been a period of unbelievable guilt and

animosity. Sometimes I listen to my mother's voice and the

things that she said only makes me sad. I can't understand why

she still treats us so coldly. It would seem by now that change

within her should have taken place. She just celebrated her

birthday and yet a will to do better is not inside her. I have a

friend whom I have not spoken to in many years, and she once

told me that her mother was mean and cruel. She made her and

other siblings get jobs at an early age in order to support the

household. Also, she put them out and told them to find their

own way before they were out of high school. Many years

went by and my friend had a child of her own and had moved

far away from her mother. She stated that a letter arrived in the

mail unexpectedly. The letter was from her mother explaining

that she was wrong for mistreating her. She said that she was

sorry and asked for forgiveness. I feel in my heart that is what

I need from my mother. I need her to ask me for forgiveness for the ugly things that she said to me, the horrible acts that took place in our home, and the many things that she made me do. My mother and I were talking recently about one of my sibling that often stayed into trouble. He is fine now that he has a relationship with God, but mama feels that he has not completely changed. She has not stated the words from her mouth, but she is always negative when speaking about him and it puts me in defense mode regarding him. She made mention that he was so bad back in the day, and I told her that he got it honest from his father. She looked at me with disbelief as to say, "How dare you speak ill of your father?" A phrase that she did say to me once that completely blew me away was "Your father wasn't that bad." I used to feel that he was the most despicable human being that lived. He had no self worth and taught me the same. He lived off the bottle and

I'm still not certain that he did not use drugs. All of his friends lived the same way and some had professional jobs. One was a firefighter and another a police officer. I don't know why my mother put up with all of the friends and their behavior. That's one thing we do not have in common. I can't and won't allow my husband's friends to come to my home and take over. I have asked Bobby's friends to leave on many occasions because of their being there was just plan wrong. I will not allow anyone to disrespect my home. One can only portray what they hear and see in their everyday surroundings. I must set the example and keep my home free from predators, profanity, drinking and destructive habits. No one will conduct themselves in a disrespectful manner upon my premises. It's not normal to have children going from house to house and being afraid to live in their own home. In reviewing these ugly memories, I have learned that in families there are no crimes that can't be forgiven. I look into the mirror and I can vividly

see the events that happened, but I feel no association. It's like

being bitten by a dog. The mean animal grips its teeth into the

skin, and it starts to bleed. After the healing process begins, it

leaves an ugly scar to remind you of what happened, but the

pain is forever gone. My mother would sometimes say that I

was just like my father. I resented her for making that

statement, because I didn't think that I had any of my father's

ways, attitude, or mannerism. He was selfish and cold-hearted

even when he wasn't drinking. I could look into his eyes and

see his soul. It was empty and he didn't have any empathy for

mankind. I don't think that he ever said the words "I'm sorry."

On his death bed, he said that he wanted to talk to my mother.

She never went to visit him. I guess she had so much hate and

anger bottled up inside that it took over her mentally and she

just couldn't bring herself to go and hear what he had to say. I never wanted to be like either of them. I can remember that she invited a family member to come from another town to live with her. He was on drugs and was using social security income in order to pay for the drugs. His check would be gone as soon as the mailman put it in the mail box. He started stealing from my mother, and she never said a word. First it was her jewelry, then money from her checking account. The amount was only $40.00 dollars, but money is money. Then the final wakeup call was when he took my sibling's television set. The neighbors saw him leaving the residence with it in his arms. Well, we could not have that. My brothers and sisters sent him on his way and told him never to return to my mother's house again. My mother never said a word. I guess she was so hurt that it left her speechless. She and my husband are so much alike in spirit. They give so much of their heart to the wrong type of people.

Chapter nineteen

I called the phone company one day to make changes to my
home phone services and the customer service representative
that answered the call said that his name was Michael. I told
him that I had a family member named Michael. He began to
ask me if I knew what the name Michael meant and I replied
no. He went on to say that Michael was an angel, one of God's
chosen, and he was one of the most beautiful angels in God's
kingdom. He said that Michael worshipped God with a pure
heart and that he spent all of his time pleasing God. He told
me that my family member was a special person in order to
have the name Michael. This conversation went on for several
minutes before we even began to discuss the reason for my
call. What made this stranger on the other end of the telephone
speak these words to me? The Michael that I knew was

nothing like the angel that he described, as a matter of fact, he was just the opposite. His demeanor was more like a wild beast living in the wilderness fighting for survival. He has no patience or self control. His vision is blurred beyond reality. He learned this hardness from the experiences he'd encountered. It was obvious that no real love or kind words were ever given in the home that he grew up in either. I know that my childhood could have been better than what it was, but there is nothing that I can do about it now. I can only teach love, give a sweet word, and speak positively to my children. I try to create a mind to follow Christ so that those dreams can come true. I ask my God in heaven to teach me to live holy and help me teach with love. I want to be changed inside and out so that my light will shine among all men. "Let your light so shine among men that they may see your good works", is what I try to practice each day. How much can one person take and does it take a lifetime in order to learn your lessons. I'm sure the answer is yes, with some people, because it's not until they're on their sickbed that they realize the wrong they have done. I have always believed that if you do good, then good will follow. I have taken a lot of pain not only from my parents who started it, but from relationships and friends. I find it so very sad that family can't get along or hate each other because of materialistic attitudes and bad tempers. It's a shame that we hold on to stuff and things to make us happy. I have never depended on things to make me happy, but my downfall was depending on people. I sometimes feel like I have been giving and giving, but gaining nothing in return. I have said "yes" when I wanted to say "no." I have come to realize that I can't make everyone accept me. There will always be people who are too selfish to share their love or anything else. What a terrible way to live in this world. It saddens me to know that the people around me have not been touched by my kindness. I love with my whole heart, and it's my desire to treat everyone that come across my path with goodness. My days are still filled with ghosts that try to steal my joy. Sometimes I think that the movie *It's a Wonderful Life"* made a grand statement when it showed that angels are always near and are what makes the world go round. Have you ever felt that way? The choices that you make forms your livelihood and puts you in a path of either positive or negative thinking, but if God was your choice from the very beginning then your life is worth the living. It amazes me to know that I have everything to live for and everything to gain. Each day I count my blessings and thank the Lord for my mindset. My grandmother used to say in her prayers that she was grateful to be clothed in her right mind. I really didn't know what that meant, but I know that it carries a lot of weight. I have watched so many family members suffer from Alzheimer's disease. The generational curses that have plagued my family and have had us bound will stop. My goal is to set the example for everyone that I come into contact with daily. I want to celebrate without having alcohol, drugs, or some type of false sense of security. I want the people around me to know that depending on anything outside of God is wrong. I watch a lot of television and have been told that I live in a fantasy world. I really don't believe that is a true statement because of my belief in the Holy Spirit.

Chapter twenty

It is written that if you trust in the Lord and obey his commandments then he will give you the desires of your heart. The day that we get married and the day that our lives end are two of the greatest events in history. Choosing a mate to share these events with will determine how it will turn out. Whether it will be bad or good is the outcome hanging in the balance.

That's why the Word says that we should be equally yoked.

Well, I'm sitting here remembering all of the terrible

Christmases that I have experienced and it happens to be that

time of year again. I guess the best Christmas that I have had

was with my grandparents thirty-five years ago. Grandmama

used to save pennies all year and then give them to my mother

to cash in and buy something for my siblings and me. She

taught me the true meaning of Christmas. I haven't yet seen

that type of love and commitment in another human being . I

have come across a lot of people in my short time, but none as

genuine as my grandmother.

Christmases that I share in my own home make me feel like I

was being punished for all the bad choices that I have made.

There is no warmth, only fake smiles and phony statements of

love. My husband doesn't like to travel on holidays or any

other time of the year. He has a hard time showing affection and doesn't care about the giving or receiving of Christmas presents. I've tried to show him that charity starts at home, and one has to show love as well as speak it from one's heart. He received his training from his parents. It seems to be common nature to be angry all the time and speak harsh words of discouragement. I was watching the movie, *A Christmas Carol,* on television one evening and my husband called the movie dumb. It involves an old man that was angry all the time and had a "bah humbug" attitude toward the Christmas holiday. He was visited by three ghosts and the last one scared him so badly that he totally changed his attitude about life. He said that he would keep Christmas in his heart for the rest of his life and he started giving with great enthusiasm. I told my husband that he needed to be visited by ghosts, but what I really meant is that he needed to change his disposition. I've never been too much of a realist. I sometimes live in a dream world. I thought of myself marrying a prince and not having anything to worry about. I watch a lot of movies like *Guess Who's Coming to Dinner and Invitation of Life,* because they tell powerful stories. I know that I have that power but I had never been able to achieve any of my dreams because fear always got in the way. I have been afraid of many things. I was afraid to learn how to drive a car but I overcame that very quickly. My mother is still afraid to drive a car, but she manages to get back and forth to work. I have never liked airplane rides and just recently this year I got over that fear. I was returning home from a distant visit with my family . It was a four hour flight. When I ride in an airplane, it always make me feel like I have no control of my body or my feelings. This strange sensation takes over me, and I'm filled with anxiety and shortness of breath. My last ride was perfect. I didn't have any type of anxiety attacks or shortness of breathe. I felt like an angel floating through the clouds in perfect peace. I have never experienced anything like it before. A calm and fearless me sat quietly in my sit thinking about how good and marvelous God is and how wonderful he has made this aircraft. Only he controls the unit that takes me from one state to another. An angel in the next seat expressed to me that you are in God's domain when you fly. You are one with him in those beautiful clouds feeling his presence keeping you safe. Why would you be afraid soaring through the clouds in the arms of your Father. "I'm gonna get my blessings. I can see it. It's on the way". These are the words to a song that I sing in the church choir. When I first heard the words they didn't mean very much, but as time went by a feeling came over me each and every time I heard it. This feeling that I couldn't shake from my soul. It stays with me day in and day out. It creates in me an unspeakable joy, and it fills my heart with gladness.

My family members call me and tell of their joys and pains.

My thoughts are incomplete when I'm talking to them, but later

on after the conversation I began to think about what I could

have said to give encouragement. I tell them how proud I am

of their accomplishments. My mother's parents often told us

how proud they were and shared in our achievements from

school. How I have wished that I had enough money to send

my siblings to college or help them in whatever field they

wanted to master. I have often said that if I had money I would

buy each one of them a home or a car. I told my mother that

one day I would have enough money to buy her a new home.

My mother has never had very much, and I don't think that she

even dreamt of having nice things. Anything is possible with

faith. The kind of faith that the eye can't see but the heart can

feel. I'm in a place where I believe in miracles. Miracles that happen in my mine and then are made tangible in my sight.

When does things and the people in your life get to be at a

point that you can say, "It is well with my soul." Does it

happen when you have a lot of money in the bank or when

everyone is grown and gone? Is it well when your issues are

taken care of and there is very little amount of stress? Is it

okay when you're so old and tired that the only thing you can

do in the mornings is wake up? Are you willing to let go of all

hurt and pain? I'm willing, and I hope and pray that it will

happen soon and very soon. Although I have experienced

verbal, physical, and mental pain that has left me hardened,

scared and lacking in self-worth, I'm willing to let go of it all.

I have heard the professionals say learn to love yourself. I do

love myself and I want only the best that my God has to offer.

We all need love although many of us have forgotten that

passage of scripture that said man should not be alone. When I first wake up in the mornings my thought is that I'm happy to be alive. My life seems so empty and unproductive until I find myself saying, "What is it that I can do from day to day that will matter or make a difference in this world?" Subsequently, I have stopped waddling in self pity and started thanking God for what I have. I remember that there are individuals worse off than I am. For instance, there are people who sleep under bridges and eat out of garbage cans. I'm not a self-starter until I overcome my fears. My motivation is fear that controls every part of me from time to time. I have a fear of being one of those people, homeless and hungry. I used to feel this way because I thought material things showed success. I have the love of a good man, and a son and daughter who have accomplished a great deal in their lives. My hopes and dreams are coming true each day that I breathe. The words that come out of my mouth are positive. My heart has been restored, and I have seen miracles beyond explanation. I listen to the voice of God telling me to still fight on. He keeps me in the midnight hour when evil presents itself. My fears become praise of worship and my prayers have been answered. He destroys the communication level with the devil and opened up his gateway to heaven. He said "Peace, be still" and I know that it was the voice of God. One night as I lay in bed about to doze off, a light flashed on in my closet. I don't have a light in my closet. Two angels came out of the closet and began to walk toward my side of the bed and one tried to pull my arm as if to take me with them. I wasn't ready to go with them, so I asked if my husband could come too and they replied, "No!" I awoke and sat up trying to analyze what just occurred. I shared this story with several people in the ministry and was told that I had heard from heaven. The pastor said that God had chosen me for a purpose and that now was the time to act. It didn't include my husband. It wasn't about family, only about me.

He wants me to walk by faith and not by sight. He told me to

lean not to my own understanding, but in all of my ways

acknowledge Him. I will put Him first in my choices and

allow Him to guide me. I asked Him to order my footsteps and

show me the way. I believe that He will carry me. I have the

wisdom that He gave me and the desire to do His will. Nothing

will separate me from the love of God. I went to church today

and after service I felt so alone and unconnected. This was the

first time that I can remember feeling this way. I have never

come from a church service wanting to just drop my head and

cry. The service touched home and filled my heart with so

many emotions. It was what I needed to hear, but I don't know

in what way that it helped my soul. I don't know why I felt so

empty. I tried to discuss it with my husband and all he could

say was to find another church to attend.   That was easy for him to say because he doesn't go to church at all. I heard a

passage of scripture, "Your thoughts are not my thoughts and

your ways are not my ways." My heart aches for those who

don't know the creator of this world. It is difficult to imagine

that there is not a God because I know that my world would

have turned out completely different. I appreciate my

childhood because it gave me a desire to seek a higher power.

The power that was given to me from the day that I was born.

That mighty power is a choice that you make in order to

become a whole person. I made that choice a long time ago,

and I stand firm by my convictions. The mean and evil people

that have crossed my path were placed there for me to tell them

that Christ could deliver them from themselves. I have raised

two children and put them on the road to glory, but I haven't

been able to show my husband that same road. I love to sing,

but I don't have a singing voice. One of my favorite spirituals is a very beautiful song called "My Living Shall Not Be in Vain." The words are, "If I can help somebody as I travel along, then my living has not been in vain. If I can show somebody that they are traveling wrong, then my living has not been in vain." I live by these words, and they keep me from falling. Although, I do fall from time to time, I continue to get up. No one ever promised me a rose garden or that my journey would be easy. I have come this far by his grace and mercy. Whenever I say my prayers, I always ask for mercy. If you only knew some of the things that I have done. You would be asking for mercy too. I have tried to live with some style and dignity and maybe that's because I have been so inhumanly degraded by so many people. First starting with home life and all of the painful memories mainly at the hands of my father. Sometimes I just wanted to go deep into a hole. The pain was so intense at times until even now when I think about it, I get nauseated. How can something that happened so long ago still affect your mind, body and soul? I know that unforgiveness can eat at the internal makeup of your body and even destroy you completely. I don't know too many people that have died from a broken heart, but I do know that it's possible. I refuse to be one of them.

Chapter twenty-one

In conclusion, this journey has carried me to many places and I have met plenty of faces. Some of the people whom I have met were walking in my shoes and understood every word that came from my mouth. Others were very kind and empathetic to my needs. There were also many who judged me for being in situations with my husband. I have heard many sermons and spoke to several therapists, but until I come to terms with the things that happened to me, none of those voices mean anything. Until I learn how to forgive myself, then and only then will change come and that change can come for you too. I have suffered through managing a household during my early years, a failed marriage, childbirth, sickness and unemployment on a regular basis. I take full responsibility for the choices I made. Sometimes I feel that I didn't choose them, but that they chose me. A statement was made that feelings don't disappear because they travel with you at any age. The mind is like a camera recording the events of time. It photographs your memories whether good or bad and stores it in a place that can be produce at a later date. One may block out the episode entirely, but something happens to bring the painful visual back to memory. It may be twenty years later and you will say, "Oh I remember that day" and it's the day pain and agony made it's way into your home. Or you view a picture taken at the age of six and think how innocent and happy you should have been. Then you wonder how you made it this far and tears roll down your face. There are tears of joy that represent the future and everything that it holds. Now is the time to let go of all of the hatred that filled your days and nights. Let go of the nightmares that resulted in sleepless nights. I will take on my fears and accept my share of the burdens and pain that I created living this life of lies and sometimes, deceit. I have asked God to forgive me for my actions, words and thoughts. I believe that He forgave me a long time ago. I want my past to go away as if it had never happened, so that I can look forward to a brand new future. If you were to ask me to describe myself in fifty words or less, here is what I would say. I'm a hopeless romantic, but I have never experienced real romance. I love all people, but I have often gotten involved with all the wrong people. I have never

really set down and made goals for myself, although I have had

many hopes and dreams. I want to become more than what I

am right now.

The journey that I'm on includes being a God fearing woman, a devoted wife, a loving Mother, and a Nana to my grandchildren loving each and every one of them unconditionally. If I can pull this off, then I will have accomplished everything in this life that I set out to do.

Made in the USA
Columbia, SC
09 March 2024

32948853R00072